SRA OPEN COURT READING

T   on

SRA

A Division of The McGraw-Hill Companies

Columbus, Ohio

www.sra4kids.com

SRA/McGraw-Hill

A Division of The McGraw·Hill Companies

Send all inquiries to:
SRA/McGraw-Hill
8787 Orion Place
Columbus, OH 43240-4027

Printed in the United States of America.

ISBN 0-07-569571-5

2 3 4 5 6 7 8 9 QPD 07 06 05 04 03 02

Table of Contents

Unit 4   Money

Unit 5   Storytelling

Unit 6   Country Life

Knowledge About Friendship

- These are some of my ideas about friendship before reading the unit.

Answers will vary.

_____

_____

_____

_____

- These are some things about friendship I would like to talk about and understand better.

Answers will vary.

_____

_____

_____

_____

   Reminder: I should read this page again when I get to the end of the unit to see how much my ideas about friendship have changed.

UNIT 1 Friendship

Recording Concept Information

As I read each selection, this is what I added to my understanding of friendship.

- "Gloria Who Might Be My Best Friend"
  by Ann Cameron

Answers will vary.

_____

_____

_____

_____

_____

- "Angel Child, Dragon Child" by Michele Maria Surat

Answers will vary.

_____

_____

_____

_____

_____

Recording Concept Information *(continued)*

- "The Tree House" by Lois Lowry

Answers will vary.

_____

_____

_____

_____

_____

_____

_____

- "Rugby & Rosie" by Nan Parson Rossiter

Answers will vary.

_____

_____

_____

_____

_____

_____

_____

- "Teammates" by Peter Golenbock

Answers will vary.

_____

_____

_____

_____

_____

_____

- "The Legend of Damon and Pythias" adapted
  by Fan Kissen

Answers will vary.

_____

_____

_____

_____

_____

_____

Recording Information: Idea Web

What do you think it takes to start a friendship?
What helps you make a new friend? Begin completing
the idea web below. Discuss and compare ideas with
your classmates. Add to the web as you read and learn
more about friendship. **Answers will vary.**

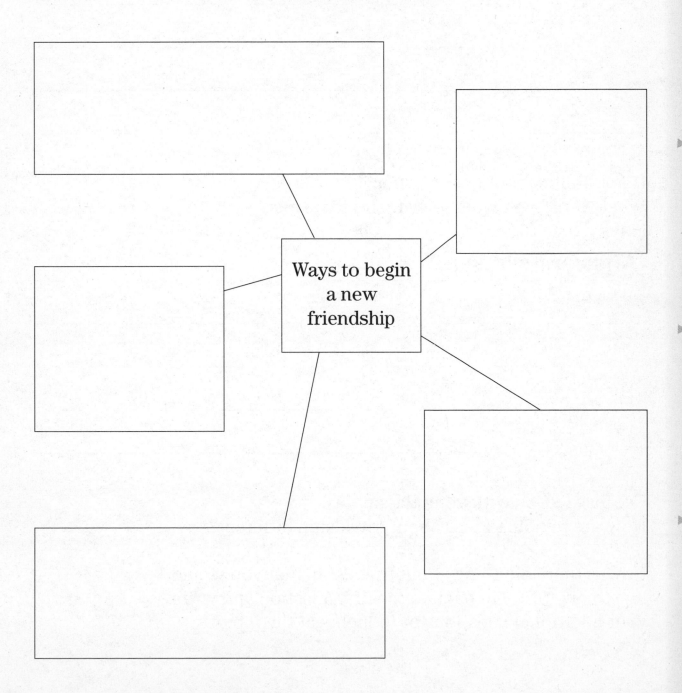

Ways to begin
a new
friendship

Recording Questions

Do you have any questions about friendship?
If so, write them here.

Answers will vary.
_____

_____

_____

_____

If not, think about this question.
What would you want your friend to be like?
Make a list.

Answers will vary.
_____

_____

_____

_____

Compare ideas with your classmates.
How are people's ideas about friendship different?

Now is there anything about friendship that you would
like to explore? Go back to the first question and write
your additional questions or thoughts at the top of
this page.

Interviewing Guidelines and Questions

Here are some guidelines to help you with your interview.

1. **Always ask permission to interview the person.** You can do this face to face, by phone, or by letter. Explain what you're doing and why. Be sure to tell him or her how much time you think you'll need.

2. **Decide ahead of time what you want to know.**

3. **Make up questions that will help you get the information you need.**

4. **Write your questions down in an organized order, leaving space between each one for taking notes.**

5. **Speak clearly and be polite.** Pay attention as the person answers.

6. **Take notes on the answers.** Jot down only enough to help you remember what the person said. You might find it helpful to use a tape recorder if one is available. Always ask the person's permission before you record his or her voice.

7. **Read over your notes as soon after you leave the interview as possible, while the conversation is still fresh in your mind.** Make additional notes to help you clarify ideas where necessary.

Interviewing Guidelines and Questions *(continued)*

Use these pages to develop questions for your family interview and for the guest speaker interview. Use the space provided to take notes on answers given during the interviews.

Questions and answers will vary.

Question: _____

_____

Answer: _____

_____

_____

_____

Question: _____

_____

Answer: _____

_____

_____

_____

Question: _____

_____

Answer: _____

_____

_____

Interviewing Guidelines and Questions *(continued)*

Question: _____

_____

Answer: _____

_____

_____

Question: _____

_____

Answer: _____

_____

_____

Question: _____

_____

Answer: _____

_____

_____

Question: _____

_____

Answer: _____

_____

_____

UNIT 1 Friendship

Project Planning Calendar

Use the calendar to help schedule your Friendship unit investigation. Fill in the dates. Make sure you mark any days you know you will not be able to work on the investigation. Choose the date on which you will start.

Sunday	Monday	Tuesday	Wednesday

Then choose the date on which you hope to finish. You may also find it helpful to mark the dates by which you hope to complete different parts of the investigation. Record what you accomplish each day.

Thursday	Friday	Saturday

Interviewing Guidelines

Rules to remember when conducting an interview:

1. **Always ask permission to interview the person.** You can do this face to face, by phone, or by letter. Explain what you're doing and why. Be sure to tell him or her how much time you think you'll need.

2. **Decide ahead of time what you want to know.**

3. **Make up questions that will help you get the information you need.**

4. **Write your questions down in an organized order, leaving space between each one for taking notes.**

5. **Speak clearly and be polite.** Pay attention as the person answers.

6. **Take notes on the answers.** Jot down only enough to help you remember what the person said. You might find it helpful to use a tape recorder if one is available. Always ask the person's permission before you record his or her voice.

7. **Read over your notes as soon after you leave the interview as possible, while the conversation is still fresh in your mind.** Make additional notes to help you clarify ideas where necessary.

Writing Questions

Make a list of some people you know who came to the United States from another country. Think about which of these people you would like to talk to about what it was like to make friends in a new country. Which ones do you think would agree to talk with you?

People I might interview: **Where they're from:**

Answers will vary.

_____   _____

_____   _____

_____   _____

_____   _____

Now think about questions that you might ask the person you interview. What do you especially want to know? Think about friendship. How will talking to this person help you learn more about friendship? Write some questions that will help you find out about friendship from the person you interview. Discuss these questions with your classmates.

Answers will vary.

_____

_____

_____

_____

Choosing Appropriate Sources

You can use the following sources to find information on a topic.

Source	Description
Atlas	A book of maps that helps you learn about a continent, country, state, or city. Atlases often have information about oceans, rivers, and mountains.
Dictionary	A reference book containing an alphabetical list of words that includes spelling, meaning, and pronunciation.
Thesaurus	A reference book containing an alphabetical list of synonyms.
Encyclopedia	A set of reference books that contains general information on many subjects. These subjects are in alphabetical order.
Magazines, Newspapers	These "periodicals" come out daily, weekly, monthly, or several times a year. Current issues contain up-to-date information.
Nonfiction Books	Nonfiction books provide facts about a topic or group of topics.
Interview	A planned conversation with a person who is an expert on a topic.
Museums and Organizations	These institutions provide information on subjects through exhibits, displays, and experts you can interview.
Internet	A network of Web sites with information on a wide range of topics.

Choosing Appropriate Sources *(continued)*

Use the list of sources on the previous page to decide where to look for the information. Write the best choice or choices on the line.

1. Where is Vietnam located?

   atlas, Internet

2. How does electricity work?

   encyclopedia, nonfiction book, museum, Internet

3. What is the definition of *cooperation*?

   dictionary

4. What damage was caused by the storm last night?

   newspaper, interview

5. Who was elected governor of our state during the last election?

   newspaper, magazine, Internet, interview

6. Where was President Lincoln born and when was he elected president?

   encyclopedia, nonfiction book, museum, Internet

7. What is another word that has the same meaning as the word *friendship*?

   thesaurus

UNIT 1 Friendship

Planning Investigation

How can you investigate friendship further? You may have already started working on a survey to investigate what people look for in a friend. Write down some other ways you can find out more about friendship.

Answers will vary.

_____

_____

_____

_____

_____

As you investigate friendship, you will want to keep a list of things you need to do. Check off each item as you complete it. Here is the start of a list of things you might want to remember to do. Add to it as you become more sure about what route your investigation will take. **Answers will vary.**

Things to Do	Completed
talk to friends	_____
talk to adults	_____
find and use books from bibliographies	_____
	_____
	_____

Planning Investigation *(continued)*

What ideas do you have for investigating and writing about friendship? What ideas about friendship would you like to explore further? Write your thoughts here. If you don't have many ideas right now, that's okay. You will probably think of more ideas as you read the rest of the stories in the unit. Add to this list each time you get a new idea.

Answers will vary.

_____

_____

_____

_____

_____

Now think of ways you can present your information to the rest of the class. Remember, you don't have to present a written report. You may choose to prepare a poster, a speech, a video, whatever you think would be the best way to present new information to your classmates. List your ideas about how to present your project. Add to this list as you read and investigate and come up with new ideas.

Answers will vary.

_____

_____

_____

_____

_____

UNIT 1 Friendship

ABC Order

ABC order, or alphabetical order, is a good way to organize lists. Look at the first letter of each word and arrange the words in ABC order. If the first letters are the same, use the letter that follows them: **st**em, **st**ick, **st**ump.

Use the lines below to write down the first names of all of the students in your class. Then on the next page, write the list of names in ABC order.

Answers will vary.

ABC Order *(continued)*

Names in ABC order:

Answers will vary.

_____   _____

_____   _____

_____   _____

_____   _____

_____   _____

_____   _____

_____   _____

_____   _____

_____   _____

UNIT 1 Friendship

Investigating Friendship

Are all of your friends the same age as you are? Think about the friends you play with at school. What about the friends on your street or in your neighborhood? Do you have family friends that you like to play with but only see once in a while?

Write the names of your friends and their ages or grades under each heading below. Some names might belong in only one list. Some might belong in two lists. Others might belong in all three lists. That's okay.

School Friends	Neighborhood Friends	Family Friends
Answers will vary.		

These are some problems I have had with friends:

Answers will vary.

Following Directions

Follow the directions to create a picture.

1. Draw a line across the box, near the bottom.

2. Draw a large square on top of the line.

3. Draw a triangle on top of the square.

4. Draw two small squares inside the box.

5. Draw a small rectangle between the two small squares.

6. Draw a circle on a stick beside the large square.

7. Color below the line green.

8. Color the circle green and the stick brown.

9. Color the large square red.

10. Color the triangle brown.

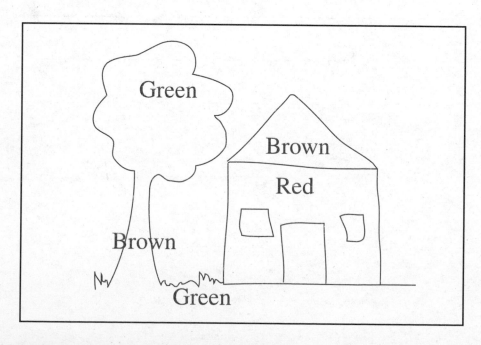

UNIT 1 Friendship

Revising Plans

What new information did we learn?

Answers will vary.

_____

_____

_____

_____

How does it help us?

Answers will vary.

_____

Does the new information lead us in any new directions for investigation? If so, what are the new questions?

Answers will vary.

_____

_____

_____

Revising Plans *(continued)*

Of the sources we have left to investigate, which
ones might answer our new questions? If none of them
will, which new sources might?

Answers will vary.

_____

_____

_____

_____

_____

Will the new questions require us to make changes
to our presentation? If so, what changes?

Answers will vary.

_____

_____

_____

_____

Parts of a Book

Knowing the parts of a book can help a reader locate information quickly and easily. Use the information below to answer the questions on the next page.

Title page
- appears at the beginning of the book
- gives the title of the book, the name of the author or editor, and the name of the publisher

Copyright page
- appears after the title page
- gives the publisher's name and the place and year in which the book was published

Table of contents
- appears in the front of the book
- lists units, chapters, or stories, along with their page numbers
- lists materials in the same order that they appear in the book

Glossary
- appears in the back of the book
- alphabetically lists new words used in the book with their definitions

Bibliography
- appears in the back of the book
- alphabetically lists books or articles the author used

Index
- appears in the back of the book
- alphabetically lists names, places, and topics in the book, with page numbers

Parts of a Book *(continued)*

1. Where would you look to find out what year the book was published? __copyright page__

2. Where would you look to find how many chapters the book has? __table of contents__

3. Where would you look to find the definition of a word from the book? __glossary__

4. Where would you look to find out what books the author used to find information? __bibliography__

5. Where would you look to find the title of the book? __title page__

6. Where would you look to see if the book has information about birds? __index__

Look in your other textbooks to see how many parts you can locate for each.

UNIT I Friendship

Unit Wrap-Up

- How did you like this unit?

  ☐ I really enjoyed it.　　☐ I liked it.

  ☐ I liked some of it.　　☐ I didn't like it.

- How would you rate the difficulty of the unit?

  ☐ easy　　　☐ medium　　　☐ hard

- How would you rate your performance during this unit?

  ☐ I learned a lot about friendship.

  ☐ I learned some new things about friendship.

  ☐ I didn't learn much about friendship.

- Why did you choose these ratings?

  Answers will vary.

  _____

  _____

- What was the most interesting thing you learned about friendship?

  Answers will vary.

  _____

  _____

- Is there anything else about friendship that you would like to learn? If so, what?

  Answers will vary.

  _____

  _____

- What did you learn about friendship that you didn't know before reading this unit?

Answers will vary.

_____

_____

_____

- What did you learn about yourself as a learner?

Answers will vary.

_____

_____

_____

- What do you need to work on to improve your skills as a learner?

Answers will vary.

_____

_____

_____

- What resources (books, films, magazines, interviews, other) did you use on your own during this unit? Which of these were the most helpful? Why?

Answers will vary.

_____

_____

_____

UNIT 2 City Wildlife

Knowledge About City Wildlife

- This is what I know about city wildlife before reading the unit.

Answers will vary.

_____

_____

_____

_____

_____

- These are some things I would like to know about city wildlife.

Answers will vary.

_____

_____

_____

_____

_____

Reminder: I should read this page again when I get to the end of the unit to see how much I've learned about city wildlife.

Recording Concept Information

As I read each selection, I learned these facts about city wildlife.

- "The Boy Who Didn't Believe in Spring"
  by Lucille Clifton

Answers will vary.

_____

_____

_____

_____

_____

_____

- "City Critters: Wild Animals Live in Cities, Too"
  by Richard Chevat

Answers will vary.

_____

_____

_____

_____

_____

_____

- "Make Way for Ducklings" by Robert McCloskey

Answers will vary.

- "Urban Roosts: Where Birds Nest in the City"
  by Barbara Bash

Answers will vary.

Recording Concept Information *(continued)*

- "Two Days in May" by Harriet Peck Taylor

Answers will vary.

_____

_____

_____

_____

_____

- "Secret Place" by Eve Bunting

Answers will vary.

_____

_____

_____

_____

_____

UNIT 2 City Wildlife

Wildlife Observation List

If you live in or near a city, or even if you live in the country, watch for wildlife that lives and survives among people. Record on these pages the kinds of wildlife that you see and any information that you think is important. Add new information to this list as you read about and investigate city wildlife.

Wildlife I Saw or Read About	Important Information
Information will vary.	

Project Planning Calendar

Use the calendar to help you schedule your
investigation for the City Wildlife unit. Fill in the dates.
Mark any days that you know you will not work on the
investigation. Choose the date on which you will start.

Sunday	Monday	Tuesday	Wednesday

Project Planning Calendar *(continued)*

Then choose the date on which you hope to finish. You may also find it helpful to mark the dates by which you hope to complete different parts of the investigation. Record what you accomplish each day.

Thursday	Friday	Saturday

Interviewing Guidelines and Questions

In an interview, you ask another person questions to get information about a subject or to find out what she or he thinks or feels about something. In an interview, a person is your source.

Use the following guidelines when conducting an interview:

1. **Always ask permission to interview a person.**

2. **Think of *who, what, when, where, why,* and *how* questions that will help you get the information you need.**

3. **Write down your questions in the order you want to ask them.**

4. **Speak clearly and be polite during the interview.** Listen carefully to the person's answers.

5. **Take notes while the person answers your questions.** Write down only enough to help you remember what the person said.

6. **Thank the person for the interview.**

7. **Read your notes as soon after the interview as possible.** That way the conversation is still fresh in your mind. Add more notes to help make the information clear.

Interviewing Guidelines and Questions *(continued)*

Imagine you are going to interview Tony from "The Boy Who Didn't Believe in Spring." Think of questions that you would ask him about spring and city wildlife. Write your possible interview questions below.

Question: **Answers will vary.**

_____

_____

Question: _____

_____

_____

Question: _____

_____

_____

Question: _____

_____

_____

Question: _____

_____

_____

Research Cycle: Problem Phase I

A good problem to research:

Answers will vary.

_____

_____

_____

_____

_____

Why this is an interesting research problem:

Answers will vary.

_____

_____

_____

_____

Some other questions about this problem:

Answers will vary.

_____

_____

_____

_____

Research Cycle: Problem Phase 2

My group's problem:

Answers will vary.

_____

_____

_____

_____

What our research will contribute to our investigation
and to the rest of the class:

Answers will vary.

_____

_____

_____

_____

Some other questions about this problem:

Answers will vary.

_____

_____

_____

_____

Research Cycle: Conjecture Phase

Our problem:

Answers will vary.

_____

_____

_____

Conjecture (my first theory or explanation):

Answers will vary.

_____

_____

_____

_____

_____

_____

_____

_____

    As you collect information, your conjectures will
change. Return to this page to record your new
theories or explanations about your research problem.

UNIT 2 City Wildlife

Wildlife Dangers Chart

Fill out this chart to keep track of how your city can be a harmful place as well as a helpful place for wildlife. Record what you already know, and add to the chart as you read and learn more.

Information will vary.

Animal Name	What is harmful in the city?	What is helpful in the city?

Research Cycle: Needs and Plans Phase I

My group's problem and conjecture:

Answers will vary.

_____

_____

_____

Write a list of things that you want to find out for your unit investigation.

- **Answers will vary.** _____

- _____

- _____

- _____

- _____

- _____

- _____

- _____

Look at the list of sources below. Decide if each will be helpful. If it will be helpful, write how it will help.

Answers will vary.

Source	Which ones?	Useful?	How?
Encyclopedias			
Books			
Magazines			
Newspapers			
Videotapes, filmstrips, etc.			
Television			
Interviews, observations			
Museums			
Internet sites			
Other			

Tables and Charts

Information can sometimes be presented in charts or tables. Charts and tables show a lot of information in a small amount of space. Information is listed in columns and rows to help you easily and quickly find specific information.

Favorite Wildlife in Our Neighborhood				
Class	**Tree**	**Insect**	**Animal**	**Wildflower**
Grade 1	white oak	ant	raccoon	goldenrod
Grade 2	maple	praying mantis	squirrel	violet
Grade 3	live oak	caterpillar	hawk	purple aster
Grade 4	blue spruce	praying mantis	raccoon	milkweed
Grade 5	sycamore	honeybee	mouse	violet

Using the chart above, answer the following questions.

1. What is the title of the chart?

   Favorite Wildlife in Our Neighborhood

2. What classes gave information for the chart?

   Grades 1–5

3. What is Grade 3's favorite animal? **hawk**

4. What is Grade 5's favorite insect? **honeybee**

5. Which two grades like the same wildflower?

   Grades 2 and 5

Natural Habitats and City Habitats Chart

As you read about and investigate city wildlife, record here what you find out about city animals' natural habitats and what they find familiar in the city.
Information will vary.

Animal	Natural Habitat	What makes it feel at home in the city?

Research Cycle: Needs and Plans Phase 2

Our problem: **Answers will vary.**

_____

_____

Knowledge Needs—Information we need to find or figure out in order to help investigate the problem:

A. **Answers will vary.** _____

B. _____

C. _____

D. _____

E. _____

F. _____

Group Members	Main Jobs

Hint: To save rewriting Knowledge Needs in the Main Jobs section, write the capital letter marking the Knowledge Need line on the Main Job line.

Using an Index

This is a page from the index of a book called *Finding Out About Our Feathered Friends*. Use it to answer the questions on the next page.

Mourning dove. *See* Dove.

National Audubon Society, The, 3, 14, 79, 85
Nests
   building, 31–42
   cleaning, 43–45, 47
   materials for, 32–35, 38, 50
   sites for, 31–33, 36, 78, 100
   See also individual birds.

Oriole, 15, 18
Osprey, 34, 48–49, 82
Owl
   description, **51,** 90–93
   mating, 25
   nests, 35
   See also Barn owl, Great horned owl.

Parakeet
   and learning, 14–16
   caring for, 15

Parrot
   imitating human speech, 19–20
   life span, 18
Passenger pigeon, 61–63, **87**
Pelican
   description, 115
   mating, 28
   migration, 65
Pigeon
   babies, 49–50
   calls, 12
   description, 61–63, **87**
   in the city, 91–92
   mating, 26
   nests, 39
   See also Dove, Passenger pigeon, Racing pigeon.

Quail, 80

Racing pigeon, **87,** 91
Raven, 13, 35, 81–82

Using an Index *(continued)*

1. How many topics are there that start with the

   letter *O*? __3__

   What are they? __Oriole, Osprey, Owl__

   _____

2. On which pages can you find information about

   Parrots? __18, 19, 20__

3. What subtopics are listed under *Parakeet*?

   __and learning, caring for__

4. What specific types of Owls does the index refer you

   to under the topic *Owls*? __Barn owl, Great horned owl__

5. Is there a listing in the index for *Ravens*? __yes__

6. On which pages can you find information about

   Materials for Nests? __32–35, 38, 50__

7. On which page can you find a description of

   a *Pelican*? __115__

8. On which pages can you find information about the

   National Audubon Society? __3, 14, 79, 85__

Disappearing Habitat Chart

Fill out the chart with information about a wildlife habitat that is threatened or gone due to city development. Record information about what has happened to the species that once lived there. Has it moved to a new home? Has its community grown smaller? Has it disappeared, too? As you come across answers in your investigation, record information here.

Information will vary.

Habitat	What's Happened to It	Species That Live There	What's Happened to Them

Note-Taking Guidelines

Note taking is an important part of investigation.

- After finding information in a book or magazine, it is important to write notes about the information.

- Note taking gives you a chance to look at your information later and review it in order to learn it and remember it.

Guidelines for Taking Notes

- Use a different page for each kind of information that you collect.

- Create a heading for each kind of information.

- Write most of your notes in your own words. Do not just copy down the author's words. Write key phrases and use abbreviations. Summarize what you have learned.

- If you want to use the author's exact words, place them in quotation marks. Also include the author's name, the book title, and the page number of the quotation.

- Write down only the most important facts and ideas about your research question or problem.

- Write neatly.

Note-Taking Guidelines *(continued)*

Use the library or the Internet to find information about Chicago, Illinois. Take notes on the information you find. You may wish to research one of the following topics:

Grant Park   Lake Michigan   Chicago River

Topic: **Answers will vary.** _____

Heading: _____

Notes: _____

_____

_____

_____

Heading: _____

Notes: _____

_____

_____

_____

Heading: _____

Notes: _____

_____

_____

_____

Diagrams

A diagram is a plan, drawing, or outline that shows how something works, that labels or explains parts of something, or that shows the relationship between parts of something.

Look at the diagram of THE TONGUE. Use the diagram to answer the questions.

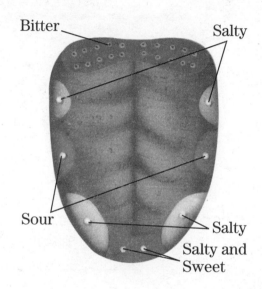

Bitter   Salty

Sour   Salty

Salty and Sweet

1. What taste bud is at the back of the tongue? **bitter**

2. What taste buds are on the tip of the tongue?
   salty and sweet

3. What taste buds are on the side of the tongue?
   sour and salty

Look at the diagram of THE EAR. Use the diagram to answer the questions.

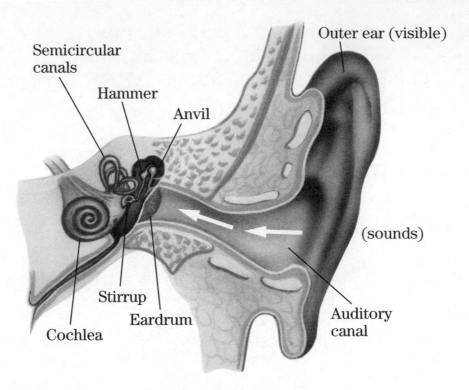

1. Name the part of the ear that you can see.

   outer ear

2. Through what part of the ear do noises enter?

   auditory canal

3. What part of the ear is farthest from the outer ear?

   cochlea

Unit Wrap-Up

- How did you feel about this unit?

  ☐ I enjoyed it very much. ☐ I liked it.

  ☐ I liked some of it. ☐ I didn't like it.

- How would you rate the difficulty of the unit?

  ☐ easy ☐ medium ☐ hard

- How would you rate your performance during this unit?

  ☐ I learned a lot about city wildlife.

  ☐ I learned some new things about city wildlife.

  ☐ I didn't learn much about city wildlife.

- Why did you choose these ratings?

  Answers will vary.

  _____

  _____

- What was the most interesting thing you learned about city wildlife?

  Answers will vary.

  _____

  _____

- Is there anything else about city wildlife that you would like to learn? What?

  Answers will vary.

  _____

  _____

- What did you learn about city wildlife that you didn't
  know before?

  Answers will vary.

  _____

  _____

- What did you learn about yourself as a learner?

  Answers will vary.

  _____

  _____

- What do you need to work on to improve your skills
  as a learner?

  Answers will vary.

  _____

  _____

- What resources (books, films, magazines, interviews,
  other) did you use on your own during this unit?
  Which of these were the most helpful? Why?

  Answers will vary.

  _____

  _____

  _____

Knowledge About Imagination

These are some of my ideas about how we use imagination before reading the unit.

Answers will vary.

_____

_____

_____

_____

_____

These are some things about imagination that I would like to talk about and understand better.

Answers will vary.

_____

_____

_____

_____

_____

Reminder: I should read this page again when I get to the end of the unit to see how much I've learned about using imagination.

UNIT 3 Imagination

Recording Concept Information

As I read each selection, this is what I added to my understanding of using imagination.

- "Through Grandpa's Eyes" by Patricia MacLachlan

Answers will vary.

_____

_____

_____

_____

_____

- "The Cat Who Became a Poet" by Margaret Mahy

Answers will vary.

_____

_____

_____

_____

_____

- "A Cloak for the Dreamer" by Aileen Friedman

Answers will vary.

_____

_____

_____

_____

_____

_____

_____

- "Picasso" by Mike Venezia

Answers will vary.

_____

_____

_____

_____

_____

_____

_____

_____

_____

- "The Emperor's New Clothes" by Hans Christian
  Andersen retold by Nadine Bernard Westcott

Answers will vary.

_____

_____

_____

_____

_____

_____

- "Roxaboxen" by Alice McLerran

Answers will vary.

_____

_____

_____

_____

_____

_____

_____

Recording Questions

Do you have any questions about imagination?
If so, write them here.

Answers will vary.
_____

_____

_____

_____

_____

If not, think about this question:
What are different ways you can use your imagination?
Make a list.

Answers will vary.
_____

_____

_____

_____

Compare ideas with your classmates.
How are people's ideas about imagination different?

   Now is there anything about imagination that you
would like to explore? Go back to the first question
and write your additional questions or thoughts at the
top of this page.

Outlining

John dropped his notecards, and now his notes on "My Day with Grandpa" are out of order. Arrange his notes and put them in the outline form below.

- Morning
- Go to bed
- Eat lunch
- Exercise with Grandpa
- Evening
- Watch television
- Get up

- Eat breakfast
- Read with Nana and Grandpa
- Eat dinner
- Afternoon
- Watch Nana sculpt
- Take a walk with Grandpa

I. **Morning**

   A. **Get up**

   B. **Exercise with Grandpa**

   C. **Eat breakfast**

   D. **Watch Nana sculpt**

   E. **Take a walk with Grandpa**

II. **Afternoon**

   A. **Eat lunch**

   B. **Read with Nana and Grandpa**

III. **Evening**

   A. **Eat dinner**

   B. **Watch television**

   C. **Go to bed**

Outlining *(continued)*

Now it is your turn to outline your day like John did. In the space below, write the correct numbers and letters to put your activities in order from morning to night.

Outlines will vary.

UNIT 3 Imagination

Project Planning Calendar

Use the calendar to help you schedule your investigation for the Imagination unit. Fill in the dates. Mark any days that you know you will not work on the investigation. Choose the date on which you will start.

Sunday	Monday	Tuesday	Wednesday

Project Planning Calendar *(continued)*

Then choose the date on which you hope to finish. You may also find it helpful to mark the dates by which you hope to complete different parts of the investigation. Record what you accomplish each day.

Thursday	Friday	Saturday

Exploring Imagination Through Poems

Title of the poem that I found: **Answers will vary.**
_____

My favorite part of the poem: **Answers will vary.**
_____

_____

_____

_____

_____

My feelings when I read this poem: **Answers will vary.**
_____

_____

_____

What I imagine when I read or hear this poem: **Answers will vary.**
_____

_____

_____

Research Cycle: Conjecture Phase

Our problem:

Answers will vary.

_____

_____

_____

Conjecture (my first theory or explanation):

Answers will vary.

_____

_____

_____

_____

_____

_____

_____

_____

_____

   As you collect information, your conjectures will
change. Return to this page to record your new theories
or explanations about your investigation problem.

UNIT 3 Imagination

Possible Sources

- Write a list of things that you want to find out about your imaginative person.

Answers will vary.

_____

_____

_____

_____

- Look at the list of sources below. Decide whether each will be helpful.

Answers will vary.

Source	Which Ones?	Useful?	How?
Encyclopedias			
Books			
Magazines			
Newspapers			
Videotapes, filmstrips, etc.			
Television			
Interviews, observations			
Museums			
Internet sites			
Other			

Planning Your Investigation

List some ideas about imagination that you would like
to investigate.

Answers will vary.

_____

_____

_____

How will you complete your investigation? **Answers will vary.**

With a partner? _____

Partner's name: _____

With a group? _____

Other members of your group: _____

_____

Check which resources you might examine while
doing your investigation. **Answers will vary.**

_____ books   _____ television

_____ encyclopedias   _____ Internet sites

_____ newspapers   _____ museums

_____ magazines   _____ art galleries

_____ other (list here) _____

_____

List books that you might want to use in your investigation.

Answers will vary.

_____

_____

_____

Explain how you plan to collect and organize your information.

Answers will vary.

_____

_____

_____

If you have information to present, think about how you might present it. Write your notes here:

Answers will vary.

_____

_____

_____

As you investigate, write down ideas that you want to remember.

Answers will vary.

_____

_____

Using a Dictionary

A dictionary can help you find a word's meaning, spelling, and pronunciation.

- The words in a dictionary are listed in ABC order, and are called **entry words.**

- At the top of each page are two words called **guide words.** The word on the left is the first entry word on the page. The word on the right is the last entry word on the page. All the words on the page fall in ABC order between these two guide words.

Look up the following words from "A Cloak for the Dreamer" in the glossary and the dictionary. Write the guide words from each source.

design

Glossary: __crop__ __environment__

Dictionary: __Answers will vary.__ _____

practical

Glossary: __post__ __royal__

Dictionary: __Answers will vary.__ _____

fashion

Glossary: __exercise__ __gutter__

Dictionary: __Answers will vary.__ _____

UNIT 3 Imagination

Exploring Imagination Through Art

These are some paintings that I have seen and like.

Title: **Information will vary.** _____

The artist is _____

I like it because _____

_____

_____

Title: _____

The artist is _____

I like it because _____

_____

_____

Title: _____

The artist is _____

I like it because _____

_____

_____

Exploring Imagination Chart

Pablo Picasso used his imagination to create paintings that forever changed art and how people looked at art. You have read about other ways in which imagination is used. On these pages, keep track of what kinds of people use their imagination and how they do it. Discuss your ideas with your classmates. Add to this chart as you read other selections in this unit and as you explore on your own.

Answers will vary. Possible answer shown.

Who uses imagination?	How do they use imagination?
1. *Pablo Picasso*	1. *He created a new style of painting.*
2.	2.
3.	3.
4.	4.

Exploring Imagination Chart *(continued)*

Who uses imagination?	How do they use imagination?
5. _____ _____ _____	5. _____ _____ _____
6. _____ _____ _____	6. _____ _____ _____
7. _____ _____ _____	7. _____ _____ _____
8. _____ _____ _____	8. _____ _____ _____
9. _____ _____ _____	9. _____ _____ _____
10. _____ _____ _____	10. _____ _____ _____

Time Lines

A time line is a graph that illustrates when things happen over time. Below are some things to remember about time lines.

- Each dot on the line represents a date.

- Each dot represents a single event.

- Events are listed on the line from left to right in order of occurrence. The earliest event appears at the far left.

- A time line can be made for any set of events; however, time lines usually show meaningful relationships among events.

- Record only important events on a time line. Avoid minor details and unimportant events.

Look back at the selection "Picasso." List seven events about Picasso's life. Then use those events to create a time line on the line provided. Be sure to include dates.

Answers will vary.

1. _____

_____

2. _____

_____

Time Lines *(continued)*

3. _____

   _____

4. _____

   _____

5. _____

   _____

6. _____

   _____

7. _____

   _____

Time lines will vary.

Exploring Imagination Chart: Interviews

Interview people you know about how their imagination has fooled them. Record what you find out on the chart below.

Name	How imagination played its trick
1. _____	_____
2. _____	_____
3. _____	_____
4. _____	_____
5. _____	_____

Have your ideas about imagination changed? Discuss your ideas with your classmates.

UNIT 3 Imagination

Investigating Imaginative Problem Solving

Write down the problem that you want to investigate.

Answers will vary.

_____

_____

How can you find out about solutions to this problem
that others have tried? List some people you can talk
to or other sources you can use.

Answers will vary.

_____   _____

_____   _____

_____   _____

What solutions did you discover for this problem?

Answers will vary.

_____

_____

_____

    Now share your thoughts about these solutions with
your classmates.

Answers will vary.

Exploring Imagination: Interviews

Write the names of the people you want to interview about the imaginary playgrounds they might have had as children. Take notes on what they tell you.

Name of person _____

Notes about what they said _____

_____

_____

_____

Name of person _____

Notes about what they said _____

_____

_____

_____

Name of person _____

Notes about what they said _____

_____

_____

_____

Exploring Imagination: Note Taking

Use these pages to take notes on the selection "Roxaboxen."

Heading: **Answers will vary.** _____

Notes: _____

_____

_____

_____

Heading: _____

Notes: _____

_____

_____

_____

Heading: _____

Notes: _____

_____

_____

_____

Exploring Imagination: Note Taking *(continued)*

Heading: _____

Notes: _____

_____

_____

_____

Heading: _____

Notes: _____

_____

_____

_____

Heading: _____

Notes: _____

_____

_____

_____

Heading: _____

Notes: _____

_____

_____

_____

UNIT 3 Imagination

Unit Wrap-Up

- How did you feel about this unit?

  ☐ I enjoyed it very much.   ☐ I liked it.

  ☐ I liked some of it.   ☐ I didn't like it.

- How would you rate the difficulty of the unit?

  ☐ easy   ☐ medium   ☐ hard

- How would you rate your performance during this unit?

  ☐ I learned a lot about imagination.

  ☐ I learned some things about imagination.

  ☐ I didn't learn much about imagination.

- Why did you choose these ratings?

  Answers will vary.

  _____

  _____

- What was the most interesting thing you learned about imagination?

  Answers will vary.

  _____

  _____

- Is there anything else about imagination that you would like to learn? What?

  Answers will vary.

  _____

  _____

Unit Wrap-Up *(continued)*

- What did you learn about imagination that you didn't know before?

Answers will vary.

- What did you learn about yourself as a learner?

Answers will vary.

- What do you need to work on to improve your skills as a learner?

Answers will vary.

- What resources (books, films, magazines, interviews, other) did you use on your own during this unit? Which of these were the most helpful? Why?

Answers will vary.

Knowledge About Money

- This is what I know about money before reading the unit.

Answers will vary.

_____

_____

_____

_____

_____

- These are some things that I would like to know about money.

Answers will vary.

_____

_____

_____

_____

_____

Reminder: When I get to the end of the unit, I should read this page again to see how much I have learned about money.

Recording Concept Information

As I read each selection, I learned these facts about money.

- "A New Coat for Anna" by Harriet Ziefert
Answers will vary.

_____

_____

_____

_____

_____

- "Alexander, Who Used to Be Rich Last Sunday" by Judith Viorst
Answers will vary.

_____

_____

_____

_____

_____

Recording Concept Information *(continued)*

- "Kids Did It! in Business" by Judith E. Rinard

Answers will vary.

_____

_____

_____

_____

_____

_____

- "The Cobbler's Song" adapted by Marcia Sewall

Answers will vary.

_____

_____

_____

_____

_____

_____

_____

Recording Concept Information *(continued)*

- "Four Dollars and Fifty Cents" by Eric A. Kimmel

Answers will vary.

_____

_____

_____

_____

_____

_____

- "The Go-Around Dollar"
  by Barbara Johnston Adams

Answers will vary.

_____

_____

_____

_____

_____

_____

- "Uncle Jed's Barbershop" by Margaree King Mitchell

Answers will vary.

_____

_____

_____

_____

_____

_____

_____

Investigation Ideas

Use this page to brainstorm ideas for your unit investigation.

Answers will vary.

_____

_____

_____

_____

_____

_____

_____

_____

_____

_____

_____

_____

The idea I've chosen to use for my unit investigation:

_____

_____

UNIT 4 Money

Possible Sources

Look at the list of sources below. Decide whether each will be helpful during your unit investigation. If it will be helpful, write how it will help.

Answers will vary.

Source	Which ones?	Useful?	How?
Encyclopedias			
Books			
Magazines			
Newspapers			
Videotapes, filmstrips, etc.			
Television			
Interviews, observations			
Museums			
Internet			
Other			

Use the lines below to write the names of books or other sources that will be helpful during your unit investigation.

Answers will vary.

_____

_____

_____

Project Planning Calendar

Use the calendar to help schedule your Money unit investigation. Fill in the dates. Make sure that you mark any days you know you will not work on the investigation. Choose the date on which you will start.

Sunday	Monday	Tuesday	Wednesday

Project Planning Calendar *(continued)*

Then choose the date on which you hope to finish. You may also find it helpful to mark the dates by which you hope to complete different parts of the investigation. Record what you accomplish each day.

Thursday	Friday	Saturday

Research Cycle: Problem Phase I

A good problem to research:

Answers will vary.

_____

_____

_____

Why this is an interesting research problem:

Answers will vary.

_____

_____

_____

_____

_____

_____

Some other questions about this problem:

Answers will vary.

_____

_____

_____

_____

_____

UNIT 4 Money

Research Cycle: Problem Phase 2

My research group's problem:

Answers will vary.

_____

_____

_____

What our research will contribute to the unit
investigation and to the rest of the class:

Answers will vary.

_____

_____

_____

_____

_____

_____

Some other questions about this problem:

Answers will vary.

_____

_____

_____

_____

_____

Ways to Earn Money Chart

There are many different ways in which children can earn money. As you read and investigate for this unit, record the different ways in which children can earn money in different places and at different times.

Answers will vary. Possible answers listed.

Ways to Earn Money	When	Where
Deliver newspapers	**after school**	**in the neighborhood**
Baby-sit	**weekends**	**at neighbors' homes or at my own house**
Rake leaves and mow lawns	**summer and fall**	**in neighbors' yards and in my yard**

Ways to Earn Money Chart (continued)

Ways to Earn Money	When	Where
Shovel snow	winter	my driveway and neighbors' driveways
Walk dogs	after school and weekends	in my neighborhood
Perform	weekends and after school	parties
Make jewelry and sell it	weekends and after school	to stores and friends

Research Cycle: Conjecture Phase

Our problem:

Answers will vary.

_____

_____

_____

_____

Conjecture (my first theory or explanation):

Answers will vary.

_____

_____

_____

_____

_____

_____

_____

_____

_____

   As you collect information, your conjecture will change. Return to this page to record your new theories or explanations about your investigation problem.

Things Worth More Than Money

Money is important both to the individual and to society, but it is not the most important thing. As you do your reading and investigations for this unit, record things that are more important than money.

Answers will vary.

I think _____

is more important than money because _____

_____

_____

I think _____

is more important than money because _____

_____

_____

Things Worth More Than Money *(continued)*

I think _____

is more important than money because _____

_____

_____

I think _____

is more important than money because _____

_____

_____

I think _____

is more important than money because _____

_____

_____

UNIT 4 Money

Research Cycle:
Needs and Plans Phase I

My group's problem:

_____

Knowledge Needs—Information I need to find or figure out in order to help investigate the problem:

A. _____

B. **Answers will vary.** _____

C. _____

Source	Which ones?	Useful?	How?
Encyclopedias			
Books			
Magazines			
Newspapers			
Videotapes, filmstrips, etc.			
Television			
Interviews, observations			
Museums			
Internet sites			
Other			

Research Cycle: Needs and Plans Phase 2

Our problem:

_____

_____

Knowledge Needs—Information we need to find or figure out in order to help investigate the problem:

A. **Answers will vary.** _____

B. _____

C. _____

D. _____

E. _____

F. _____

Group Members	Main Jobs

Comparing Information Across Sources

Good writers use the most reliable sources available. To make sure that information is correct, cross-checking between sources is sometimes necessary.

To make sure that your sources are reliable, consider the following points:

- Is the source written by an expert? Book jackets and notes at the beginning or end of articles sometimes give information about the authors.

- Is the source up-to-date? Would another source be more up-to-date?

- Is the information detailed enough?

- Is the information relevant to the topic?

Sources you might have used:

Encyclopedias	Books	Magazines
Newspapers	Videos	Interviews
Personal Experiences	Museums	Internet

Comparing Information Across Sources *(continued)*

Think about your unit investigation. On the lines below, list the sources that you are using. Then, write what other sources you can use to check the information that you received from the original sources.

Source used: __Answers will vary._____

Sources to check against: _____

_____

Source used: _____

Sources to check against: _____

_____

Source used: _____

Sources to check against: _____

_____

Source used: _____

Sources to check against: _____

_____

Source used: _____

Sources to check against: _____

_____

UNIT 4 Money

Varieties of Money Chart

Many different things have been used as money across the ages. As you read the selections in this unit and as you do your investigation, record the names of things that have been used as money, and when and where they were used.

Answers will vary.

Things Used as Money	When	Where

Diagrams

Look at the diagram of the front of a one-dollar bill below. Identify the six features that the diagram displays and designates with boxes. Use the letter of the answers below to label each box. The first one has been done for you.

A. Picture of George Washington

B. Seal and letter of the Federal Reserve Bank that issued the note

C. Value of the note (one of four places where it appears)

D. Year when the note was designed

E. Serial number (one of two places where it appears)

F. Signatures of the Treasurer of the United States and the Secretary of the Treasury

UNIT 4 Money

Time Lines

A time line is a graph that illustrates when things happen over time. Below are some things to remember about time lines.

- Each dot on the line represents a date or time.

- Each dot represents a single event.

- Events are listed on the line from left to right in the order they occurred. The earliest event appears at the far left.

Imagine you are going to the zoo. List five things below that you would like to do while you are there. Then, on the time line, show the order in which you would do the things.

Answers will vary.

_____

_____

_____

_____

●   ●   ●   ●   ●
5:00   5:30   6:00   6:30   7:00

Unit Wrap-Up

- How did you feel about this unit?

  ☐ I enjoyed it very much.   ☐ I liked it.

  ☐ I liked some of it.   ☐ I didn't like it.

- How would you rate the difficulty of the unit?

  ☐ easy   ☐ medium   ☐ hard

- How would you rate your performance during this unit?

  ☐ I learned a lot about money.

  ☐ I learned some new things about money.

  ☐ I didn't learn much about money.

- Why did you choose these ratings?

Answers will vary.

_____

_____

_____

- What was the most interesting thing you learned about money?

Answers will vary.

_____

_____

_____

_____

_____

- What did you learn about money that you didn't know before?

  Answers will vary.

_____

_____

_____

- What did you learn about yourself as a learner?

  Answers will vary.

_____

_____

_____

- What do you need to work on to improve your skills as a learner?

  Answers will vary.

_____

_____

_____

- What resources (books, films, magazines, interviews, other) did you use on your own during this unit? Which of these were the most helpful? Why?

  Answers will vary.

_____

_____

_____

_____

Knowledge About Storytelling

- These are some of my ideas about storytelling before reading the unit.

  Answers will vary.

  _____

  _____

  _____

  _____

  _____

- These are some things I would like to know about storytelling.

  Answers will vary.

  _____

  _____

  _____

  _____

Reminder: I should read this page again when I get to the end of the unit to see how much I've learned about storytelling.

UNIT 5 Storytelling

Recording Concept Information

As I read each selection, this is what I added to my understanding of storytelling.

- "A Story A Story" retold by Gail E. Haley
Answers will vary.

_____

_____

_____

_____

_____

- "Oral History" by T. Marie Kryst
Answers will vary.

_____

_____

_____

_____

_____

_____

Recording Concept Information *(continued)*

- "Storm in the Night" by Mary Stolz

Answers will vary.

_____

_____

_____

_____

_____

_____

- "Carving the Pole" by Diane Hoyt-Goldsmith

Answers will vary.

_____

_____

_____

_____

_____

_____

_____

- "The Keeping Quilt" by Patricia Polacco

Answers will vary.

- "Johnny Appleseed" by Steven Kellogg

Answers will vary.

- "Aunt Flossie's Hats (and Crab Cakes Later)"
  by Elizabeth Fitzgerald Howard

Answers will vary.

Folktales

Use this page to write down the folktales that you have read.

Folktale: **Answers will vary.** _____

Summary: _____

_____

_____

Folktale: _____

Summary: _____

_____

_____

Folktale: _____

Summary: _____

_____

_____

Folktale: _____

Summary: _____

_____

_____

UNIT 5 Storytelling

Questions to Explore

I would like to find answers to these questions about storytelling:

1. **Answers will vary.** _____

   _____

   _____

2. _____

   _____

   _____

3. _____

   _____

   _____

Where I might go to find the answers:

Answers will vary. _____

_____

_____

Following Directions

Directions tell you how to do something. Practice following directions by completing the steps below.

1. Take out crayons or colored pencils.

2. Draw a hat on the spider's head and color the hat red.

3. Draw a feather sticking out of the hat. Color the feather yellow.

4. Draw a shoe on each of the spider's eight feet.

5. Color all the shoes on the left side blue.

6. Color all the shoes on the right side purple.

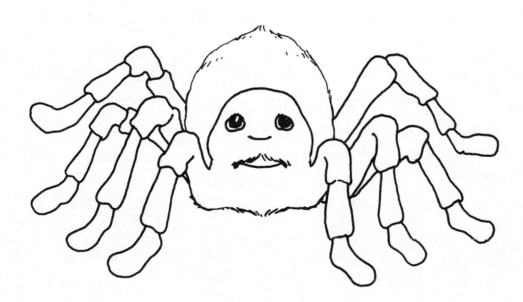

Name_____ Date_____

Project Planning Calendar

Use the calendar to help schedule your investigation for Storytelling. Fill in the dates. Mark any days you know you will not work on the investigation. Choose the date on which you will start.

Sunday	Monday	Tuesday	Wednesday

Then choose the date on which you hope to finish. You may also find it helpful to mark the dates by which you hope to complete different parts of the investigation. Record what you accomplish each day.

Thursday	Friday	Saturday

UNIT 5 Storytelling

Planning Your Investigation on Storytelling

List some ideas about storytelling that you would like to investigate.

Answers will vary.

_____

_____

_____

_____

How will you complete your investigation?

With a partner? **Answers will vary.** _____

Partner's name: _____

With a group? _____

Other members of your group: _____

_____

Check which resources you might examine while doing your investigation.

_____ books   _____ television

_____ encyclopedias   _____ Internet sites

_____ newspapers   _____ museums

_____ magazines   _____ art galleries

_____ other (list here) _____

Planning Your Investigation on Storytelling *(continued)*

List books that you might want to use in your investigation.

Answers will vary.

Explain how you plan to collect and organize your information.

Answers will vary.

If you have information to present, think about how you might present it. Write your notes here:

Answers will vary.

As you investigate, write down ideas that you want to remember.

Answers will vary.

UNIT 5 Storytelling

Questions for Family Storytellers

Use this page to write down what you would like to learn about when you talk to a family member. Then, turn your statements into questions you can ask your family members.

What I would like to learn about:

Answers will vary.

_____

_____

_____

_____

What questions I could ask to help me find the information I need:

Answers will vary.

_____

_____

_____

_____

How Stories Are Passed On Chart

As you read and explore storytelling, write down ways you discover that stories can be passed on. Tell the importance, interest, or value of each.

Answers will vary. Possible answer is given.

How Stories Can Be Passed On	Importance, Interest, or Value of Each
a totem pole	*keeps stories of a tribe* *it's beautiful* *maintains a tribe's heritage*

Internet Searches

Logical Operators Use these simple words (commands) to make your search more specific.

The most commonly used operators are *and, or,* and *quotation marks.*

How It Works

- If you are looking for information on tribes in Washington, then enter **tribes AND Washington.** The search engine will then look for sources that have both of these words.

- If you are looking for information on Adena and Blackfoot Indians, enter **Adena OR Blackfoot,** and the search engine will pull up sources with one or the other term (instead of only those sources that contain both words).

- Put quotation marks around specific names. For example, to find information on Flint Ridge, enter **"Flint Ridge"** in the search box of the search engine. (Otherwise, the search engine will show you all the articles that have the words *flint* and *ridge* in them. That can mean a lot of searching!)

Practice coming up with key words and using logical operators. Read the following items and fill in the blanks.

Internet Searches *(continued)*

1. You are looking for information about the growing season of Washington apples.

   Key Words: **Washington apples**

   Logical Operator: **"Washington apples"**

2. You are looking for folklore from Brittany.

   Key Words: **folklore   Brittany**

   Logical Operator: **folklore and Brittany**

3. You would like more information about totem poles.

   Key Words: **totem poles**

   Logical Operator: **"totem poles"**

4. You would like to learn about tribes from the Ohio Valley.

   Key Words: **tribes   Ohio   Valley**

   Logical Operator: **tribes and "Ohio Valley"**

5. You would like more information on the Pacific and Atlantic Oceans.

   Key Words: **Pacific Atlantic Ocean**

   Logical Operator: **"Pacific Ocean" or "Atlantic Ocean"**

Name _____ Date _____

Storytelling Objects Web

As you read about, investigate, and discuss storytelling, record on this page objects that you discover can be used to tell and pass on stories. Fill in a web for each item you find out about. Add to the webs as you read more. Create more webs on your own as you need and discuss more objects.

Answers will vary. Possible answers given.

The big fire

A big parade

Hats

Storytelling Objects Web • Inquiry Journal

Name _____ Date _____

A Class "Keeping" Object

Discuss ideas for a "keeping" object that you and your classmates might make to tell the story of the year you have spent together. Record your ideas and plans below.

What will the "keeping" object be? **Answers will vary.**

_____

_____

_____

_____

These are materials we might use: **Answers will vary.**

_____

_____

_____

_____

These are stories we might tell: **Answers will vary.**

_____

_____

_____

_____

UNIT 5 Storytelling

Exploring Legends

Think about other legendary people you have heard about, such as Paul Bunyan, Davy Crockett, Pocahontas, Annie Oakley, and Pecos Bill.

Conduct an investigation to discover the true facts behind the legend.

Legendary character: **Answers will vary.** _____

True facts: **Answers will vary.** _____

_____

_____

_____

_____

Legendary character: **Answers will vary.** _____

True facts: **Answers will vary.** _____

_____

_____

_____

_____

Legendary character: **Answers will vary.** _____

True facts: **Answers will vary.** _____

_____

Family Story Objects

Write down any summaries of stories you remember or have heard passed on. Write down summaries of family stories that revolve around a special family object.

1. **Answers will vary.** _____

_____

_____

_____

_____

2. _____

_____

_____

_____

_____

3. _____

_____

_____

_____

_____

UNIT 5 Storytelling

Using the Dictionary

Dictionaries contain different kinds of information, including spellings, pronunciations, and meanings, or definitions. The words are listed in ABC order.

Use a dictionary to select the correct definition of the words listed below. Circle the correct answer for each word.

1. **trillion**

   a. a very tiny number

   b. (a very large number)

   c. a number equal to zero

   d. a noise that a bird makes

2. **terrapin**

   a. something you put in your hair

   b. a large furry animal

   c. the pin that holds the wheel on a bicycle

   d. (a type of turtle)

3. **rescue**

   a. (to save or free)

   b. a pool stick

   c. place where a baby takes a nap

   d. a very small dog

Unit Wrap-Up

- How did you feel about this unit?

  ☐ I enjoyed it very much. ☐ I liked it.

  ☐ I liked some of it. ☐ I didn't like it.

- How would you rate the difficulty of the unit?

  ☐ easy ☐ medium ☐ hard

- How would you rate your performance during this unit?

  ☐ I learned a lot about storytelling.

  ☐ I learned some new things about storytelling.

  ☐ I didn't learn much about storytelling.

- Why did you choose these ratings?

  Answers will vary.

  _____

  _____

- What was the most interesting thing you learned about storytelling?

  Answers will vary.

  _____

  _____

- Is there anything else about storytelling that you would like to learn? What?

  Answers will vary.

  _____

- What did you learn about storytelling that you didn't
  know before?

  Answers will vary.

  _____

  _____

  _____

  _____

- What did you learn about yourself as a learner?

  Answers will vary.

  _____

  _____

  _____

  _____

- What do you need to work on to improve your skills
  as a learner?

  Answers will vary.

  _____

  _____

  _____

  _____

- What resources (books, films, magazines, interviews,
  other) did you use on your own during this unit?
  Which of these were the most helpful? Why?

  Answers will vary.

  _____

  _____

  _____

Knowledge About Country Life

- This is what I know about country life before reading the unit.

Answers will vary.

_____

_____

_____

_____

_____

- These are some things I would like to know about country life.

Answers will vary.

_____

_____

_____

_____

_____

Reminder: I should read this page again when I get to the end of the unit to see how much I have learned about country life.

Recording Concept Information

As I read each selection, I learned these new facts about country life.

- "The Country Mouse and the City Mouse"
  by Aesop

Answers will vary.

_____

_____

_____

_____

_____

- "Heartland" by Diane Siebert

Answers will vary.

_____

_____

_____

_____

_____

_____

_____

- "Leah's Pony" by Elizabeth Friedrich

Answers will vary.

- "Cows in the Parlor: A Visit to a Dairy Farm"
  by Cynthia McFarland

Answers will vary.

Recording Concept Information *(continued)*

- "Just Plain Fancy" by Patricia Polacco

   Answers will vary.
   _____
   _____
   _____
   _____
   _____

- "What Ever Happened to the Baxter Place?"
   by Pat Ross

   Answers will vary.
   _____
   _____
   _____
   _____
   _____

- "If you're not from the prairie…" by David Bouchard

   Answers will vary.
   _____
   _____
   _____
   _____

Investigation Ideas: Country Life

Use this page to brainstorm ideas for your unit
investigation activity.

Answers will vary.

_____

_____

_____

_____

_____

_____

_____

_____

_____

_____

_____

The idea I've chosen to use for my unit investigation:

_____

_____

UNIT 6 Country Life

Interviewing About Country Life

People to interview: _____ Answers will vary. _____

_____

_____

_____

What I would like to find out: _____ Answers will vary. _____

_____

_____

_____

_____

Questions I would like to ask: _____ Answers will vary. _____

_____

_____

_____

_____

_____

_____

Name _____ Date _____

Project Planning Calendar

Use the calendar to help schedule your Country Life unit investigation. Fill in the dates. Make sure that you mark any days you know you will not work on the investigation. Choose the date on which you will start.

Sunday	Monday	Tuesday	Wednesday

Then choose the date on which you hope to finish. You may also find it helpful to mark the dates by which you hope to complete different parts of the investigation. Record what you accomplish each day.

Thursday	Friday	Saturday

Research Cycle: Problem Phase I

A good problem to research:

Answers will vary.

_____

_____

_____

_____

_____

Why this is an interesting problem:

Answers will vary.

_____

_____

_____

_____

_____

Some other questions about this problem:

Answers will vary.

_____

_____

_____

_____

UNIT 6 Country Life

Research Cycle: Problem Phase 2

My group's problem:

Answers will vary.

_____

_____

_____

_____

_____

What our research will contribute to the unit
investigation and to the rest of the class:

Answers will vary.

_____

_____

_____

_____

Some other questions about this problem:

Answers will vary.

_____

_____

_____

Research Cycle: Conjecture Phase

Our problem:

Answers will vary.

_____

_____

_____

_____

Conjecture (my first theory or explanation):

Answers will vary.

_____

_____

_____

_____

_____

_____

_____

_____

_____

_____

_____

   As you collect information, your conjecture will change. Return to this page to record your new theories or explanations about your research problem.

UNIT 6 Country Life

Types of Farms Web

Many types of farms exist. You have read about several types in this unit. As you do your reading and investigations for this unit, list the different types of farms you learn about. Make information webs about the farms. Record interesting facts about each one. Add pictures from magazines or draw your own.

Answers will vary. Possible answers shown.

milking machines

cows

dairy farm

silos

milk

calves

community

old-fashioned

barn raising

Amish farm

speak German dialect

cornhusking party

not rich

harvest in October

potato farm

hard work

use school kids

soybeans

chickens

alfalfa

milk

farm business

woods

barley

corn

Types of Farms Web • Inquiry Journal

Types of Farms Web *(continued)*

UNIT 6 Country Life

Research Cycle:
Needs and Plans Phase I

My group's problem: **Answers will vary.** _____

_____

_____

Knowledge Needs—Information I need to find out or figure out in order to help investigate the problem:

A. **Answers will vary.** _____

B. _____

C. _____

Source	Which ones?	Useful?	How?
Encyclopedias			
Books			
Magazines			
Newspapers			
Videotapes, filmstrips, etc.			
Television			
Interviews, observations			
Internet sites			
Museums			
Other			

Graphs

Study the graph. Fill in the circle next to the correct answer for each question.

Favorite Dessert

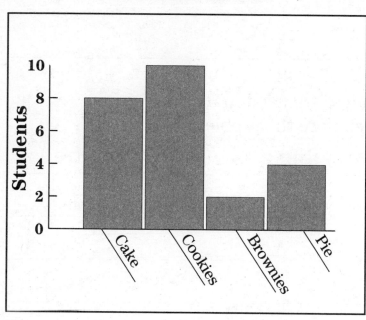

Based on a class poll of 24 students.

1. What is the title of the graph?
   ○ 24 students ● Favorite Dessert ○ Best Desserts

2. How many students liked brownies?
   ● 2 ○ 4 ○ 8

3. How many students were in the class?
   ○ 8 ● 24 ○ 10

4. What was the class's favorite dessert?
   ○ pie ○ brownies ● cookies

5. What was the class's least favorite dessert?
   ● brownies ○ cookies ○ cake

UNIT 6 Country Life

Research Cycle:
Needs and Plans Phase 2

My group's problem: _____**Answers will vary. Possible answer:**_____

What is it like to live on a farm?

_____

Knowledge Needs—Information we need to find out
or figure out in order to help explore the problem:

A. __**Answers will vary. Possible answers: What does a**__

B. __**farm have on it? What work has to be done on a**__

C. __**farm?**_____

D. _____

E. _____

F. _____

Group Members	Main Jobs

Seasonal Activities in the Country Chart

To people who live in the country, the seasons of the year are very important. Often, their work and their other activities are determined by the seasons. As you do your reading and investigations for this unit, use the chart below to keep track of what you learn about seasonal chores and other activities in the country. To get you started, a few entries have been made in the chart. You do not need to fill in all the blanks for every person or group you list.

Person or Group	Chores or Activities			
	Spring	**Summer**	**Autumn**	**Winter**
Leah's family	**Plant seeds**		Harvest seeds, sell crop, pay back bank loan for seeds	
Naomi and Ruth		**Hold frolics-quilting** **Care for chickens**		
Baxter family	Plant crops	**Works in the fields** **Milks the cows**	**Preserve vegetables, take vegetables and eggs to market**	

Note Taking

Read the paragraph and the questions that follow it. Fill in the circle next to the best answer to each question.

Hieroglyphics is a system of writing in which pictures are used instead of words or letters. The Egyptians are the most famous users of hieroglyphics. Other people, like the Maya, also used hieroglyphics. Scientists believe the Egyptians began using hieroglyphics more than 5,000 years ago. Hieroglyphics were carved on stone or written on something like paper. We can understand hieroglyphics because of the Rosetta Stone. This stone has hieroglyphics and other languages on it. People were able to translate from the hieroglyphics to the other languages.

1. If you were taking notes about the meaning of the word *hieroglyphics*, which of these would be most important?
   ○ Egyptians used hieroglyphics.
   ● Hieroglyphics is a form of picture writing.
   ○ Sometimes hieroglyphics were carved on stone.

2. If you were taking notes about understanding hieroglyphics, which of these would be most important?
   ● The Rosetta Stone helped us understand hieroglyphics.
   ○ Hieroglyphics are more than 5,000 years old.
   ○ The Maya used hieroglyphics.

Unit Wrap-Up

- How did you feel about this unit?

  ☐ I enjoyed it very much. ☐ I liked it.

  ☐ I liked some of it. ☐ I didn't like it.

- How would you rate the difficulty of the unit?

  ☐ easy ☐ medium ☐ hard

- How would you rate your performance during this unit?

  ☐ I learned a lot about country life.

  ☐ I learned some new things about country life.

  ☐ I didn't learn much about country life.

- Why did you choose these ratings?

  Answers will vary.

  _____

  _____

- What was the most interesting thing you learned about country life?

  Answers will vary.

  _____

  _____

  _____

  _____

  _____

- What did you learn about country life that you didn't know before?

  Answers will vary.

- What did you learn about yourself as a learner?

  Answers will vary.

- What do you need to work on as a learner?

  Answers will vary.

- What resources (books, films, magazines, interviews, other) did you use on your own during this unit? Which of these were the most helpful? Why?

  Answers will vary.